DERMOT TURING

ALAN TURING
THE LIFE OF A GENIUS

FOREWORD

BY PROFESSOR ANDREW BLAKE, DIRECTOR OF THE ALAN TURING INSTITUTE

WRITING IN THE 21ST century, the so-called 'age of algorithms', it is difficult to comprehend just how radical some of the ideas of Alan Turing were in 1950 when he first wrote about a 'thinking machine'. And yet we now confront this phenomenon in our everyday lives, in our smartphones, how we shop and travel, how we move around cities. It is thanks to Turing and others of his generation, making fundamental theoretical breakthroughs in computing, that we now see such rapid progress in machine learning techniques and artificial intelligence.

As a mathematician, making theoretical leaps while also turning his mind to solving real-world problems, Turing is the very exemplar of the principles that a new national centre named in his honour, The Alan Turing Institute, is here to champion. Created to lead research into data science, its goal is to advance the world-changing potential of this new science. In the same way that Turing and his colleagues were brought together at Bletchley Park to answer a national need, in his case breaking the famous Enigma code, The Alan Turing Institute was created in 2015 to answer a national need for data science, benefitting government, industry and society.

For modern-day scientists and engineers, honouring Turing's legacy, it is our job to live up to the standards of courage and excellence he has set for us, and honour the huge impact of his work that he sadly never lived fully to see. We aspire to do him justice.

INTRODUCTION

TODAY ALAN TURING IS a well-recognised name, but it was not always so. Until the last few years of the 20th century hardly anyone had heard of him or his achievements.

All that changed when the British government, very gradually, permitted the story of what had happened at Bletchley Park during the Second World War to emerge. Not only did we discover that the Allies had successfully broken the Axis powers' codes throughout the war, but we learned that Alan Turing had had a pivotal role in breaking the Enigma cipher, which was used by all German forces and in all theatres for the whole of the war.

And then there are Alan's other achievements. What he did at Bletchley Park may be the best-known, but Alan's intellectual leadership went far wider. Alan Turing is the man who conceived the idea of a programmable computer, who invented the discipline of artificial intelligence, and proposed a chemical theory about shape and form in living things. The list of things on his CV is so long that, in 1970, when nothing was known about Bletchley Park, mathematicians referred to Alan's time out for the war as 'wasted years'.

Once it became known that Alan Turing's personal story was, in a way, a Shakespearian tragedy – despite his achievements, he had been convicted of something which in most people's minds should never have been a crime, and shortly afterwards took his own life – people took Alan Turing to their hearts.

I hope you will enjoy finding out a little more about this very remarkable man.

The author, Sir Dermot Turing.

Dermot's uncle, Alan Turing, sits in a rocking chair during his 1937 stay in America.

FAMILY BACKGROUND, CHILDHOOD & SCHOOLDAYS

ALAN TURING WAS BORN on 23 June 1912 in Maida Vale, North London. Perhaps he had no business being born in Britain at all: Alan's father, Julius Turing, was in the Indian Civil Service, and India was where Alan's brother John had been born four years before. With Alan's arrival, it was time for the big decision: where should the family be brought up? Like so many others, Julius and Alan's mother Ethel decided to find a foster family to look after John and Alan in Britain while they went back to duty in Madras.

Thus Alan spent his childhood years with a military family called the Wards. He was the youngest of a big brood, natural and foster children all mixed together, and it was a good place to grow up. Alan could mess about with what interested him, with only a modicum of military discipline being applied from time to time. And it was becoming clear that what interested him was not the rough-and-tumble of pillow fights with the below-stairs staff, but things going on in the natural world. It was good that Alan showed promise; but it would have been so much better if he had been a bit tidier, and come to table with clean fingernails and brushed hair.

Below: Alan as a young child.

Below, right: Alan, aged about four, with his father and brother, outside the Wards' house.

School might put that right. Hazelhurst Preparatory School continued the Wards' approach of letting Alan do his own thing, and it did not do much to tidy him up. There was a tradition of making the boys do practical things for themselves, with plenty of carpentry and other hands-on activities. Alan's letters to India described various inventions – not least a homemade fountain pen, which must have dismayed the school laundry.

After Hazelhurst was Sherborne School, chosen for its modern approach to science and mathematics. By now, Julius and Ethel had left India and the family were living in France, meaning that Alan had to get to his new school by cross-Channel ferry. Alan made his mark on the first day: the 1926 General Strike had broken out, and in the absence of trains Alan decided, aged 13, to cycle all the way to Sherborne, a distance of some 60 miles.

The initial admiration for Alan's feat didn't last. His school reports were not exactly positive. Summer Term, 1927: 'Mathematics. Not very good. His work is dirty.' Michaelmas Term, 1927: 'House Report. I don't care to find him boiling heaven knows what witches' brew by the aid of two guttering candles on a naked window sill.' Alan's brother John said that when their father received Alan's reports, it was a good time to be out of the house.

Above: **Nowell Smith** was the headmaster at **Sherborne School** while Alan was there.

Below: Alan (far left) with other boys from Hazelhurst School in 1925.

SCHOLARS & KING'S

SOMETHING CHANGED BY 1928. Alan had waded through Einstein's Theory of Relativity and provided Ethel Turing with a blotchy 32-page précis of it. Now he was in the sixth form and could explore in detail the subjects that interested him, whether it be the behaviour of planets, the chemistry of iodates or the appearance of fungi in a beaker. Most significantly, Alan found someone he could talk to about these things: Christopher Morcom. Christopher was in the year above and became both mentor and friend. But, quite suddenly, Christopher died of tuberculosis. He was only 18.

Right: Alan walking down the street in Guildford in 1934.

Below: Alan's teddy bear, Porgy.

Christopher's death could have knocked Alan sideways, but it doesn't seem to have done so. Alan set up a recreation of Foucault's pendulum in his boarding house at Sherborne, demonstrating the rotation of the earth; he wrote a witty fake formula for an edition of the school magazine to show younger students how to achieve a pass in their Latin exam through eating iced buns; and he scraped together enough tidiness to do well in his own Cambridge entrance exam. Alan also began a lasting relationship with Christopher's mother, who was filling a gap in his life just as he was in hers.

Alan arrived at King's College, Cambridge, in the autumn of 1931. Although Alan did not know it yet, he had entered a secret society – five members of the King's high table had worked for the British government's most clandestine organisation of the First World War, the codebreaking organisation called Room 40.

For the time being, Alan threw himself into ordinary undergraduate pursuits: rowing, beer, and not doing terribly well in his first-year exams. That result ashamed him, and by the time he finished his degree course he had scored a distinction in the special 'Schedule B' paper only taken by the brightest mathematicians. This meant that his degree was marked 'B-star' – giving Alan a moment of amusement when he thought his aunts might 'write congratulatory letters on getting a "B"'. He also had the confidence to ask his mother to give him a teddy bear for Christmas. A bizarre request, perhaps; but as Alan said, he'd never had one as a child – it was one of those things that had been overlooked, with the parents so far away in India.

Alan's rowing trophies.

ENTER THE MACHINES

ALAN WAS ALLOWED TO stay on at Cambridge for an extra year, taking an advanced course in the foundations of mathematics, for which the lecturer was Max Newman. Newman was describing a problem which had the mathematicians of the early 1930s scratching their heads. The question was whether there is a mathematical litmus test to apply to mathematical theorems: in other words, can you know beforehand if it's worth spending the time sweating over a proof. This unsolved question was called the *Entscheidungsproblem*.

Above: Max Newman.

Below: A model 'Turing machine'.

Newman explained that the issue was whether there was a mechanical process – 'I may even have said, a machine can do it' – to determine whether theorems can be proved. He hadn't expected to be taken literally. But Alan Turing, a mere student, decided to do just that. In his most famous mathematical paper 'On Computable Numbers, with an Application to the *Entscheidungsproblem*', Alan set out the idea of a multipurpose machine, whose function would be changed according to the instructions it was given. This concept of a programmable computer became known as the 'Turing machine'. And along the way, Alan demolished the *Entscheidungsproblem* – he proved there was no litmus test for mathematical theorems.

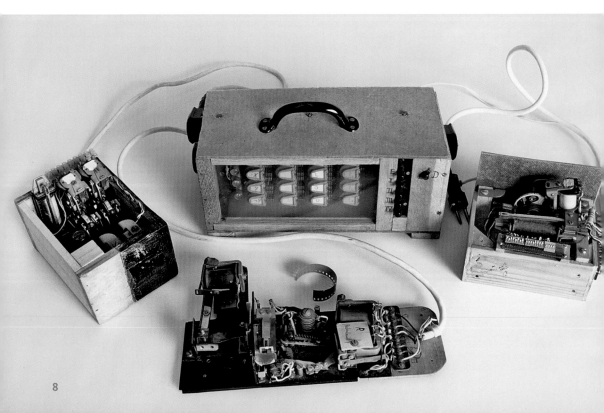

Alan's reputation as a mathematical logician was now established. He had become a Fellow of King's, and was now going to Princeton University to study alongside Alonzo Church, one of the leading thinkers in his specialist field.

Mathematical logic at Princeton could have been an uncongenial experience, partly because Alonzo Church was a man of fastidious habits and partly because Alan found the different culture of America hard to adjust to. But soon enough he'd made some new friends, and by his second year he was making a multiplication machine. Back in Cambridge in 1938, he began work on another machine to find solutions to a specific mathematical problem, which involved illicit trips to the engineering labs to cut brass gearwheels. The wheels were all different, as the number of teeth had to be prime numbers. Parts of the machine were scattered about the floor of Alan's rooms, much to the bewilderment of his visitors.

Some of the visitors were rather important. Alan had come back to Britain, rather than taking up a permanent job he'd been offered at Princeton, because another war with Germany was on the horizon. The important visitors had that in mind too, and they had a job for Alan, which would need all his ingenuity, logic, and practical hands-on approach to engineering.

Above: A schematic for the machine Alan was building in 1938 using brass gearwheels.

Below: Princeton University, where Alan carried out research from 1936–38.

ENIGMA

THE VISITORS WERE PROFESSOR Frank Adcock, a veteran of Room 40 and a Fellow of King's, and Alastair Denniston, the head of Britain's secret Government Code & Cypher School, which was the successor to Room 40. They were recruiting talent, not just because they foresaw another war with Germany, but because technological developments meant they needed a new generation of codebreakers.

Sir Frank Adcock, in the rain at King's College, Cambridge.

Disguising messages sent in Morse code had become mechanised during the late 1920s, and Britain was behind the game. The immediate challenge was the Enigma machine, which could be set up in any one of 158.9 million million million ways to encipher a message. Without knowing the set-up, called the 'key', the Germans' military messages were going to remain a secret. But Commander Denniston had other plans.

Recognising that machines and mathematics should be brought to bear on the new mechanical ciphers, his idea was to create a list of mechanically minded mathematicians 'of the professor type' to call upon if war broke out. And who better than Alan Turing, a mathematician already known for the 'Turing machine', with proven ability to turn theory into reality.

Alan (second from right) with Fred Clayton (left) and Jewish refugees in 1939.

Alan leaped at the chance, and was sent off to a basic codes and ciphers course in London in early 1939. He was tutored in the operation of the Enigma machine by Dilly Knox, another Room 40 veteran and, of course, another Fellow of King's.

Meanwhile, the international situation was deteriorating. Another friend from King's, Fred Clayton, was sponsoring a Jewish refugee boy who had arrived in Britain, and Fred encouraged Alan to do likewise. Alan helped to find a school place and accommodation for another refugee, and as the storm clouds gathered over Europe in the summer of 1939, the four of them had a boating holiday in Chichester. One might need some imagination to gauge the success of this venture, given Alan's complete lack of experience with sailing craft of any kind.

Germany invaded Poland in September 1939, and the professors on Denniston's reserve list were called in. The place they were told to report to was an unprepossessing country house on the outskirts of an unprepossessing town. Its main advantages were that the railway station was right next door to the house and that nobody had heard of the place. Alan Turing was going to spend the war at Bletchley Park.

Below, left: A Second World War German Enigma machine.

Below, right: German soldiers encipher a message on an Enigma machine during the Second World War.

11

BLETCHLEY & THE BOMBE

'Prof's book', an introduction to Enigma written by Alan for new codebreakers.

BACK IN 1932, A team of mathematicians and engineers in Poland had unmasked the secrets of the Enigma machine. In great secrecy they had found ways to identify the 'key' – the way the Enigma machine was set up to send and receive messages, which could be changed as often as every day. One technique used a machine they called the 'bomba'. Alastair Denniston and Dilly Knox had been invited to Warsaw in July 1939, where they had been let in on the Enigma secret, given a copy of a rebuilt Enigma machine, and shown the workings of the bomba.

When Alan Turing turned up at Bletchley Park on 4 September 1939, his priority job was to find a method of *revealing* the secret key, enabling encrypted messages to be read. Alan's idea was to rig up as many Enigma machines as possible, and test whether there was an Enigma setting at which an expected German stock military phrase was transformed into the intercepted message. Alan's Enigma-busting machine was called the 'bombe' out of respect to its Polish progenitor.

The bombe was up and running and finding keys by the time of the Battle of Britain in 1940. From that point on, German army and air force Enigma messages were no secret from the Allies, and deciphered Enigma messages

A captured German U-boat in 1942.

had significant influence in the Battle of Britain, in the war at sea, and in the North African campaign (to name just a few).

Some of the people working at Bletchley Park found Alan Turing's unmilitary behaviour a little unusual: the most famous story is of Alan wearing his gas mask when cycling in to work as a protection against hay fever. And it's also said that he chained his mug to the radiator to prevent it from being stolen. Although he was never a professor, Alan's friends at Bletchley called him 'Prof' because he seemed to fit the caricature.

His friends included Joan Clarke, a rarity at Bletchley because she was a female codebreaker. Thousands of women worked at Bletchley, but only a handful ranked alongside the men in senior positions. She and Alan, being intellectually well-matched, grew close and were even engaged for a while in 1941; but Alan explained to her that he had 'homosexual tendencies' and after a few months he called it off.

Although he was put in charge of Hut 8, the division of Bletchley Park responsible for naval codebreaking, Alan was a poor administrator and it was obviously right to find him another role.

Above: **Alan's one-time fiancée, Joan Clarke.**

Below: **The bombe.**

SECOND WORLD WAR

ALTHOUGH IT IS NOW well known that Alan Turing spent the first few years of the war as a codebreaker, what he was involved in after about 1942 is much more obscure. His work on the Enigma problem had largely been completed in the early years, and by 1942 Bletchley Park had turned into an intelligence factory. Inventive mathematicians like Prof didn't fit well into the industrial structure that the Park had now become.

Some things have, however, come to light. In 1942 Alan was sent on a highly secret mission to the United States. In part the objective was to pass on know-how to the Americans, who were designing a special bombe with electronic components to deal with a new type of Enigma machine installed in U-boats, which had four rather than three rotors. But it was also to report on various new technological developments going on across the Atlantic.

Codebreakers from Bletchley Park's Hut 6, after moving into a new building in 1943.

Alan's first mission in the US was to examine and report on a new teleprinter encipherment device: you typed in your text, and instead of a regular telex message going out over the airwaves, a scrambled version was substituted. At the receiving end, the cipher was reversed and the clear text would print out. Alan's new job was to check the security of this device.

It wasn't just typed messages that were being encrypted. There was the much more difficult issue of phone calls. The scrambler that President Roosevelt and Winston Churchill relied on used amateur-grade security, so the Germans had been happily listening in to their conversations for some time. The Americans had nailed the problem, though, with an invention called X-61753. Alan Turing was ordered by the British to inspect and report on the security of X-61753.

There was only one problem. X-61753 was secret and the Americans weren't going to allow a British civilian near their secret laboratory. The British threatened to pull out of the UK-US 'special relationship' for intelligence-sharing unless Alan was admitted to see the strange machine. The Americans yielded, and Alan was allowed in.

The secret phone-call machine was secure enough. But it weighed 50 tons and needed 13 people to operate it, and its output was a horrible screech. On his return to Britain, one of Alan's new research projects was to produce something that did the same job but in a more practical way. His workplace was no longer to be Bletchley, but an equally secret establishment a few miles away – the Radio Security Service at Hanslope Park.

The US Navy's bombe designed to deal with the four-rotor Enigma machine used in U-boats.

DELILAH, COLOSSUS, & THE PUB

ALAN'S HANDS-ON STYLE was all very well, but his technical accomplishment fell a little short of the standards expected by the experts around him. Donald Bayley was a young lieutenant in the Royal Engineers assigned to work on Alan's compact scrambler:

> This chap had his shirt hanging out. There were resistors and capacitors, as fast as he'd soldered one on another would fall off. It was a spider's nest of stuff ... He was annoyed I mentioned his shirt hanging out.

Another co-worker was Robin Gandy, also a mathematics graduate from King's and Alan's future best friend. Robin named the phone-call machine 'Delilah' because he said that the biblical Delilah was a deceiver of men.

Alan Turing didn't have to work full time on his soldering project. The authorities at Bletchley Park still had a use for him, in a committee that also included Max Newman. Newman was leading the attack on the Germans' own teleprinter cipher. Like Enigma, the challenge was to find out how the teleprinter encipherment had been set up, and, once again, machinery was going to be used to tackle it. This time they were going to use electronics: huge banks of vacuum-tubes, rather like small light bulbs, would do the job that previously had been the preserve of mechanical parts and electrical relays. The codebreaking machine was so big they called it 'Colossus'.

Above: Robin Gandy, a lifelong friend of Alan's.

Below: World Chess Champion Garry Kasparov tries to beat the IBM Deep Blue chess computer in 1997.

Alan Turing's role in the building of Colossus was peripheral; with his other responsibilities he was more of a consultant than a designer, and the engineering was being done by Tommy Flowers from the General Post Office. Colossus was a much more interesting machine than a bombe: it could be reset with switches to carry out different tasks. The codebreakers at Bletchley Park soon realised that they were handling a programmable electronic device. It was, very nearly, a computer. When there was downtime from codebreaking, the codebreakers tried to get Colossus to do long multiplication.

In the pub at Wolverton, which is halfway between Hanslope and Bletchley, Alan might be found playing chess with Donald Michie, one of the Colossus team. Several of the codebreakers were grand masters, but neither Alan nor Donald were in that league. What they were talking about was how you might write a program to get a machine to play chess. For, with the advent of Colossus, the future was clear. Programmable computing machines were going to be a reality in the post-war world.

The Colossus at the
National Museum of
Computing: almost the
world's first computer.

ACE & ATHLETICS

ALAN TURING'S LAST DUTY of the Second World War was a secret visit to an installation in Germany – the Laboratorium Feuerstein, in a remote castle in Bavaria. Here the Germans had been working on a collection of highly secret projects, including the encryption of phone calls and the development of modern computing machinery. The Allies chose Alan and Tommy Flowers to inspect these efforts. What they saw was not particularly impressive, but they could use the time to talk about the future.

Above: **Alan with his running mates from Walton Athletic Club, 1946.**

Below: **The ACE computer under construction.**

The grand plan of the late 1940s was to build a programmable electronic computing machine. Alan was taken on by the National Physical Laboratory (NPL), where by December 1945 he had written up a full design for a computer. The machine was going to be called 'ACE' – the Automatic Computing Engine – in homage to Charles Babbage's Difference and Analytical Engines of the previous century.

But there was a wide gulf between the design on paper and the delivery of an actual machine. Months and months went by. Perhaps, it was suggested, they should build a smaller 'pilot' machine just to see if it would work? (Of course it would work; anyone who had seen Colossus knew that. But the people in charge hadn't seen Colossus, and the people who had were bound

by the Official Secrets Act.) Alan didn't approve of the pilot machine idea because it wouldn't be powerful enough to work on any really interesting problem. Alan Turing needed to find something else to do.

In fact, Alan had been filling his spare time with long-distance running. It was the period leading up to the 1948 Wembley Olympics and in track events Britain was expecting to do quite well. Alan was recruited by the Walton Athletic Club:

> We heard him rather than saw him. He made a terrible grunting noise when he was running, but before we could say anything to him, he was past us like a shot out of a gun. A couple of nights later, we kept up with him long enough [to invite] him to join Walton. He did and immediately became our best runner.

In 1946 Alan won the three-mile Club Track Championship and in 1947 he came fifth in the Amateur Athletic Association Championship Marathon. His marathon time (2 hours 46 minutes) wouldn't be impressive by today's standards, but it was good enough then for him to be considered for the Great Britain Olympic squad. Alan was 35 at the time, though, and a leg injury put paid to that idea.

Amateur Athletic Association

18th Southern Championships

WHITE CITY STADIUM
Saturday, July 6 1946

OFFICIAL PROGRAMME SIXPENCE

Above: A race programme cover from 1946.

Below: Alan Turing was an Olympic-standard runner in 1947.

ROBOTS & SCRAP-IRON

Above: **Sir Charles Darwin, Director of the NPL.**

Below: **The members of the Ratio Club. Alan Turing is seated, on the left.**

CONSTRUCTION OF THE ACE did not begin until 1954 and it was not finished until 1958, by which time it was already out of date. Long before then, Alan's ideas were heading in a new direction. 'Turing is going to infest the countryside with a robot which will live on twigs and scrap-iron!' said one colleague at the NPL.

Well, not exactly. Science fiction and boys' magazines of the late 1940s were full of ideas about robots and rockets and electronic brains – and Alan's plans for a computing machine, even one that had yet to be built, went far beyond the mundane problems that its sponsors had in mind. They had assumed that computing was about calculating – doing difficult arithmetical problems and solving equations, for example in working out how to fire a surface-to-air missile accurately. Alan thought this much too restrictive. He still wanted to get a computer to play chess, but it went further than that. Alan's aims didn't fit in with the mission of the NPL, as his boss Sir Charles Darwin (the grandson of *the* Charles Darwin) wrote:

> As you know Dr. A. Turing ... has designed the theoretical part of our big computing engine. This has now got to the stage of ironmongery, and so for the time the chief work on it is passing into other hands ...

and we are agreed that it would be best that Turing should go off it for a spell.

Or, to decode the message: Alan could have a sabbatical year to work on a paper about Intelligent Machinery. He thought it possible that machines could learn from their experiences – and that artificial intelligence was plausible. For Sir Charles Darwin this was schoolboy fantasy and he dismissed Alan's paper as 'not fit for publication'. The paper – now recognised to be a foundation of artificial intelligence – was not published for another 20 years.

There was another reason why Alan's colleagues at NPL thought he was going to build a robot. Around this time, in 1949, Alan joined the Ratio Club, a group of scientists who were thinking about control. They were debating how animals control their movements based on what their senses tell them, and they were asking how this related to the way commands in computers control the actions of the machine. To test their ideas some members of the Ratio Club had, well, built robots. And, to the irritation of Alan Turing, elsewhere in Britain some people had already built a working computer.

Below, left: **The mind as a machine.**

Below: **George the robot with his creator, Tony Sale.**

THE 300-YEAR-OLD SUM

WHILE ON HIS SABBATICAL year, Alan bumped into Max Newman again. After the war, Newman had set up his own computer laboratory at Manchester University. In 1948 he told Alan Turing that his own pilot machine was up and running. Then Newman sweetened the pill. Alan was offered a job – to become Deputy Director of Newman's lab.

Max Newman's machine was in fact a rather untidy accumulation of wires and spare parts from Colossus, which he had somehow cadged when the war ended and Bletchley Park was being disbanded. Its memory size was meagre (1,024 bits), which meant that only very limited programs could be run. The room it was housed in was tiled in brown Victorian brick (described by one Manchester professor as the 'late lavatorial' style) and faintly radioactive.

One problem the machine could work on was a theorem from the 17th century concerning prime numbers. To crank out the long division by hand was unbelievably tedious and likely to be inaccurate. The machine could do it; but the idea of an artificial brain was not to everybody's taste.

Sir Geoffrey Jefferson, the country's leading neurologist and brain surgeon, found out what was going on in the brown brick room and used the opportunity of a speech at an awards ceremony to express his dismay: 'Not until a machine can write a sonnet or a concerto because of thoughts and emotions felt could we agree that machine equals brain. When we hear it said that wireless valves think, we may despair of language.'

The Times wanted a comment on Sir Geoffrey's speech to accompany its breathless report on the mechanical brain's 'Answer to 300 year old sum'. The reporter spoke to Alan Turing, who said:

> This is only a foretaste of what is to come, and only the shadow of what is going to be. I do not see why it should not enter any one of the fields normally covered by the human intellect, and eventually compete on equal terms. I do not think you can even draw the line about sonnets, though the comparison is perhaps a little bit unfair because a sonnet written by a machine will be better appreciated by another machine.

Above: Sir Geoffrey Jefferson, who debated with Alan whether machines could think.

Opposite, below: Max Newman's 'mechanical brain' at Manchester University, pictured in *The Times* in 1949.

All this was a bit much for Max Newman, who was driven to send in a letter explaining just how boring the computer actually was. The problem was not just that Alan had sensationalised the machine, but now the wild idea of machinery that could 'think' was out in the open.

THE UNIVERSITY OF MANCHESTER

commemorates

ALAN MATHISON TURING
1912-1954

A Creator of Computer Science,
Code Breaker and Mathematician

Reader in Mathematics
1948-1954

The Rutherford Building
at Manchester University,
where Newman had
his lab. A blue plaque
commemorates Alan
Turing's role at Manchester.

THE TURING TEST

ALAN TURING HATED WRITING up his mathematical and scientific papers for learned journals. But Robin Gandy said there was one paper that Alan really had enjoyed doing – his 1950 paper on 'Computing Machinery and Intelligence'. Alan begins this paper with the words, 'I propose to consider the question "Can machines think?"' – and then he demolishes, one after the other, the grumbles and objections of sceptics like Sir Geoffrey Jefferson.

Alan's paper sets out a simple test for deciding whether a machine can think: you hide it behind a screen and ask it questions. If you think it's a human, it's probably thinking. The 'Turing Test' is now firmly established (and still criticised) in the study of artificial intelligence, and annual competitions are run to see if a computer program can beat the judges. Oddly, developments in technology now require internet shoppers and others to identify themselves as humans by deciphering wonky text – a task that is beyond the capabilities of computers; or, to put it another way, the computer is applying a reverse Turing Test to see if the user is a human or another program.

Above: **The Turing Test.**

Right: **Captcha is a Completely Automated Public Turing test to tell Computers and Humans Apart.**

i'm a captcha!

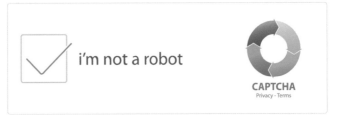

i'm not a robot

CAPTCHA
Privacy - Terms

Eps10 vector

Type the two words:

CAPTCHA
Privacy - Terms

In 1950 computer programs were still primarily about calculation, and few other applications had been imagined except for the sorting of data in an office environment. The idea of a machine 'thinking' was thus controversial, but it was also great fun: Alan, Max Newman and Sir Geoffrey were invited to have a debate about it on the radio; and even today there are debates about the effectiveness of machine learning and what machines can do, what humans can do, and where the dividing lines might be.

Alan Turing was settling in at Manchester. He had become a Fellow of the Royal Society and a Reader at the university; he had bought a house for the first time; and he was a welcome guest with various friends, particularly those with children with whom he had a special rapport. William Newman, Max's young son, famously trounced Alan in the game of Monopoly. William's version of the game had an extra street running diagonally across the board.

Below, left: William Newman's bespoke Monopoly board.

Below: Alan Turing in the mid-1930s.

Meanwhile, at work, Alan was spending his research time on a biological problem, but this was nothing to do with brains or the meaning of thought. His new project was even more fundamental. It was about the very shape of living things.

MORPHOGENESIS

FROM HIS EARLIEST CHILDHOOD days, when he had been immersed in Rudyard Kipling's *Just So Stories*, Alan had been intrigued by the question of developing shape in animals and plants. But this was a real, unsolved problem: embryos are spherical and something was needed to explain how the symmetry was upset. Even if you imagined a chemical diffusing across the surface of the sphere, it was inadequate to explain changes of shape. Alan Turing was not shy to state the obvious: 'It certainly cannot result in an organism such as a horse, which is not spherically symmetrical.'

Alan's paper about spherical symmetry and horses presented a new approach, involving two chemicals diffusing and reacting with each other. These could be modelled with differential equations – equations that would be horrible to solve using pencil-and-paper methods, but which, with the arrival of the sparkling full-size Manchester Mark 1 computer in February 1951, became a problem in programming, which Alan Turing was rather good at.

Alan Turing stands next to the brand-new Mark 1 computer in Manchester.

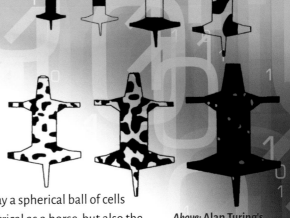

Alan's equations could explain not just the way a spherical ball of cells could turn itself into something as unsymmetrical as a horse, but also the stripes on a zebra and the blotching on a Friesian cow, the arrangement of florets in sunflowers and daisies, and even the arrangement of leaves on a stem and the spirals around a fir cone.

On 8 February 1952 Alan was due to go to London to present his 'Chemical Theory of Morphogenesis' to the Ratio Club. But the day before he was due to speak, Alan Turing's world fell to pieces.

Above: Alan Turing's equations provide a theory for how patterns form on animal skins.

Below: The same ideas applied to seeds in a sunflower head (left) and leaf buds on a plant stem (right).

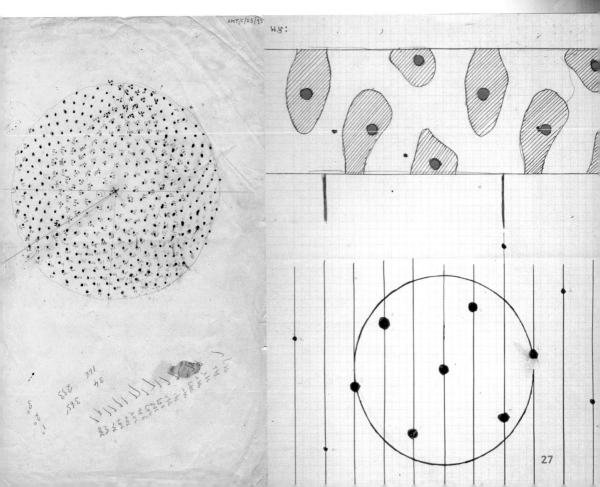

THE BURGLARY

IN EARLY 1952 ALAN'S house had been burgled. Various things, most of them of little importance but of some value, had been taken. So Alan did what people do when they are burgled: he went to the police, which was the worst decision of his life.

What the police found suspicious was how Alan seemed to know the identity of the culprit: the burglar was a miscreant friend of Arnold Murray, and Arnold was a young man that Alan had met in a pub and taken home. These facts only raised questions about what Arnold had been doing in Alan's house in the first place. For under the criminal law of the 1950s, it was illegal for men to have consensual sex together, in private, and if the police were right, there had been another offence that they could count towards their clear-up statistics.

Alan Turing was committed to appear before the Knutsford Quarter Sessions at the end of March 1952. He pleaded guilty and his lawyers devised a strategy that could help him avoid a prison sentence, a criminal record and the loss of his job; they planned to convince the judge to put Alan on probation. There would be a condition, however, which was for Alan to 'submit to treatment by a duly qualified medical practitioner'.

The gold-plated spoon that Alan's mother said was proof that he died accidentally. Alan used potassium cyanide for gold-plating and his mother had warned him about getting the chemical on his hands.

The judge took the course suggested and Alan kept his job. What none of them realised was that 'treatment' would include not just a few sessions with a psychiatrist, but also the implantation of an oestrogen substitute. The sessions with the psychiatrist went well, though they revealed Alan's fractious relations with his mother; the hormone treatment had unpleasant side effects.

While Alan continued to work on the application of his morphogenesis theory to plants and single-cell sea creatures – and he seemed to have got through the course of treatment with good humour – there are indications that in 1954 all was not well. The immediate cause is still unclear, but on 7 June 1954 Alan Turing took a huge dose of cyanide and died in his own bed. Also found at the scene was an apple, partly eaten in order to mask the taste of the poison.

Some controversy continues as to whether Alan's act was deliberate or an accident. But the accident theory was deliberately put about by John, Alan's brother, to shield their mother from the full facts; she firmly adhered to the accident idea for the rest of her life.

Messages from the Unseen World '54 AMT/D/4/14

? Don't the psychic what desired?

III The Universe is the interior of the Light Cone of the Creation

IV Science is a Differential Equation. Religion is a Boundary Condition

Arthur Stanley

AMT/D/4/16
1954

V Hyperboloids of wondrous Light
Rolling for aye through Space and Time
Harbour there Waves which somehow Might
Play out God's holy pantomime.

'Messages from the Unseen World': postcards sent by Alan shortly before he died reveal a more whimsical side of his character.

University Reader Sent For Trial With Another Man

AT a special court in Wilmslow on Wednesday, Alan Mathison Turing (39), F.R.S., single, University reader, of Adlington Road, Wilmslow and Arnold Murray (19), unemployed, Boncarn Drive, Wilmslow, were committed for trial at Knutsford Quarter Sessions on March 31, on three charges of gross indecency.

Detective Constable Robert Wills said he went to Turing's home with Detective Sergeant Rimmer on February 7. He said to Turing: "On February 3 you visited Wilmslow Police Station and gave information about two men, who you alleged, had broken into your house. We have made inquiries, and now have some information. Would you please give us his description?" Turing replied: "He's about 25 years of age, 5 ft. 10 inches, with black hair".

Constable Wills said: "We have reason to believe your description is false. Why are you lying?"

AN AFFAIR

A. M. Turing.

Turing, it was alleged replied: "I tried to mislead you about my informant. I have been an accessory to an offence in this house. I have had an affair with him and I have regarded his conduct as a form of blackmail and have consulted my solicitor about him. His name is Arnold Murray. I picked him up in Oxford Street, Manchester.

Constable Wills read out a statement alleged to have been made by Turing in which he said he had committed an offence at his home with Murray.

In an alleged statement Murray said he met Turing in Oxford Street and "knew what he was by the way he talked".

Turing told him he worked on the Electronic Brain at Manchester University. The statement gave details of alleged offences at Turing's home on three dates.

MATERIALLY CORRECT

When a copy of Murray's statement was served on Turing he was alleged to have said: "The statement is materially correct".

Turing reserved his defence and Murray said he had nothing to say.

Turing was allowed £50 bail, but Murray was remanded in custody. Murray was granted legal aid.

Alan's committal was reported in the *Alderley and Wilmslow Advertiser* on 29 February 1952.

Alan's house in Wilmslow (on the left).

ALAN TURING'S LEGACY

ALAN TURING IS RENOWNED for many different reasons. All sorts of things get named after him, ranging from ring roads to investment funds, and there are statues, websites, plays, blue plaques and even oratorios in his name. He has been described as the father of computing and artificial intelligence, and he is best known for his work on Enigma at Bletchley Park. His work on morphogenesis is less well known, but has had a recent revival as present-day experiments have validated his theories about diffusion and the reaction of biochemicals in developing animals. He is also remembered for the treatment he suffered at the hands of the justice system in 1952.

The formal apology by Gordon Brown.

Remarks of Prime Minister Gordon Brown
10 September 2009

This has been a year of deep reflection – a chance for Britain, as a nation, to commemorate the profound debts we owe to those who came before. A unique combination of anniversaries and events have stirred in us that sense of pride and gratitude that characterise the British experience. Earlier this year, I stood with Presidents Sarkozy and Obama to honour the service and the sacrifice of the heroes who stormed the beaches of Normandy 65 years ago. And just last week, we marked the 70 years which have passed since the British government declared its willingness to take up arms against fascism and declared the outbreak of the Second World War.

So I am both pleased and proud that, thanks to a coalition of computer scientists, historians and LGBT (lesbian, gay, bisexual and transgender) activists, we have this year a chance to mark and celebrate another contribution to Britain's fight against the darkness of dictatorship: that of code-breaker Alan Turing.

Turing was a quite brilliant mathematician, most famous for his work on breaking the German Enigma codes. It is no exaggeration to say that, without his outstanding contribution, the history of the Second World War could have been very different. He truly was one of those individuals we can point to whose unique contribution helped to turn the tide of war. The debt of gratitude he is owed makes it all the more horrifying, therefore, that he was treated so inhumanely.

In 1952, he was convicted of "gross indecency" – in effect, tried for being gay. His sentence – and he was faced with the miserable choice of this or prison – was chemical castration by a series of injections of female hormones. He took his own life just two years later.

Thousands of people have come together to demand justice for Alan Turing and recognition of the appalling way he was treated. While Turing was dealt with under the law of the time, and we can't put the clock back, his treatment was of course utterly unfair, and I am pleased to have the chance to say how deeply sorry I and we all are for what happened to him. Alan and the many thousands of other gay men who were convicted, as he was convicted, under homophobic laws, were treated terribly. Over the years, millions more lived in fear in conviction. I am proud that those days are gone and that in the past 12 years this Government has done so much to make life fairer and more equal for our LGBT community. This recognition of Alan's status as one of Britain's most famous victims of homophobia is another step towards equality, and long overdue.

But even more than that, Alan deserves recognition for his contribution to humankind. For those of us born after 1945, into a Europe which is united, democratic and at peace, it is hard to imagine that our continent was once the theatre of mankind's darkest hour. It is difficult to believe that in living memory, people could become so consumed by hate – by anti-Semitism, by homophobia, by xenophobia and other murderous prejudices – that the gas chambers and crematoria became a piece of the European landscape as surely as the galleries and universities and concert halls which had marked out the European civilisation for hundreds of years.

It is thanks to men and women who were totally committed to fighting fascism, people like Alan Turing, that the horrors of the Holocaust and of total war are part of Europe's history and not Europe's present. So on behalf of the British government, and all those who live freely thanks to Alan's work, I am very proud to say: we're sorry. You deserved so much better.

Gordon Brown

In 2009 Prime Minister Gordon Brown issued a formal apology to Alan Turing for his mistreatment, and in 2013 the coalition government led by David Cameron arranged a Royal Pardon, effectively cancelling his conviction. The Royal Pardon created controversy of its own, as approximately 50,000 other men who were convicted of the same offence might justly point out that their cases are no different. Alan Turing's legacy may be to stand as a proxy for all of them.

I suspect that Alan himself would have abhorred the fuss and hero status with which he is now regarded. He kept his OBE medal in his toolbox and grumbled when they put 'OBE' after his name on his office door at NPL. There are stories of him trying to hide from even the small-scale celebrity status he had achieved in academic circles from writing that famous piece 'On Computable Numbers' back in 1936. He was probably happiest when sitting in the garden with his next-door neighbours' little boy discussing whether God could catch a cold if He sat on damp grass. So, if Alan's story is able to inspire young people today to achieve remarkable things, I think he would be happy with that as his legacy.

PLACES TO VISIT

Bletchley Park
The Mansion
Bletchley Park
Sherwood Drive
Bletchley
Milton Keynes MK3 6EB
Tel: 01908 640404
www.bletchleypark.org.uk

The National Museum of Computing
Block H
Bletchley Park
Milton Keynes MK3 6EB
Tel: 01908 374708
www.tnmoc.org

Science Museum
Exhibition Road
South Kensington
London SW7 2DD
Tel: 020 7942 4000
www.sciencemuseum.org.uk

Museum of Science and Industry
Liverpool Road
Manchester M3 4FP
Tel: 0161 832 2244
msimanchester.org.uk

Imperial War Museum London
Lambeth Road
London SE1 6HZ
Tel: 020 7416 5000
www.iwm.org.uk

Imperial War Museum North
The Quays
Trafford Wharf Road
Manchester M17 1TZ
Tel: 0161 836 4000
www.iwm.org.uk